A POUND OF
Butter

GORDON PLANEDIN

WORKBOOK PRESS LLC
187 E Warm Springs Rd,
Suite B285, Las Vegas, NV 89119, USA

Website: https://workbookpress.com/
Hotline: 1-888-818-4856
Email: admin@workbookpress.com

Ordering Information:
Quantity sales. Special discounts are available on quantity purchases by corporations, associations, and others. For details, contact the publisher at the address above.

Library of Congress Control Number:
ISBN-13:   978-1-96075-221-5 (Paperback Version)
              978-1-960752-22-2 (Digital Version)

REV. DATE: 03/28/2023

A POUND OF
Butter

GORDON PLANEDIN

DEDICATION

*To my sweetheart Mary with thanks given
for the help of my daughter Karen and my grandson
Gordon Shaw.*

Contents

Foreword

IF YOU WERE TO go to a store to buy a pound of butter you would take the butter off the shelf and taking it to the cashier you would pay for the butter. If the price was five dollars per pound you would pay the five dollars and take it home. There would be an empty space on the shelf but soon someone would replace that pound and all is well with no damage to anyone.

If you were to take someone's life then there would be a very empty space on many people's shelves and the very tragic part is that those spaces cannot be easily refilled if they can be refilled at all. The loss to those of the empty spaces is so great that it is unimaginable and we all know that the loss will go on forever.

So, the value of a pound of butter is five dollars. What is the value of a life?

The simple and obvious answer is a life, which is the full price. Therefore, if you take someone's life you should be prepared to forfeit your own. There are obviously excuses and exceptions, unavoidable accidents, honest mistakes, etcetera, but there has to be a price to pay. If you kill someone because you were driving like a fool, drunk or otherwise, this is not an honest mistake. No matter how you try to explain it to the victim's family. If you sell drugs to someone in order to provide yourself with a good lifestyle and the drug addicts destroy their lives this is not an honest mistake, and so on and so forth.

The bottom line is that if you are not prepared to pay the full price then please leave the butter on the shelf!

HE WAS A QUIET looking average man in average looking clothes sitting there quietly on a bench as if waiting on an appointment. He had a shopping bag on his lap and a pleasant smile on his face. The lady at the reception desk after only a brief glance totally ignored him. However, when Israel Micheal Sukinsin walked through the entrance doors there was nothing average about him. A little taller than most and a couple of extra pounds but after that it was obvious to everyone that he was a mover and that he knew that very well himself, almost to the point of arrogance. He picked up his mail from the lady at the reception desk and turning on his heel he headed for his office in the corner of the building. Mr. Average guy joined him just a few steps from the door whereupon Izzy turned to him intending to promptly send him on his way. Mr. Average guy standing next to Izzy so that their backs were to the lobby opened up the top of his shopping bad and Izzy could plainly see the twin barrels of a 12 gauge sawed off shotgun staring him in the eyes. The man's right hand was in the shopping bag so the message was very clear. Izzy's mouth dropped open and he was about to ask a question when Mr. Average nodded slightly towards the office and in a quiet but firm voice said "Let's get inside." Since Mr. Sukinsin already had the remote control in his hand it was a simple matter to press the button for the pocket door to slide into the wall and for them to step inside.

Once inside and acting on instructions the door slid closed, and the remote control was laid onto Izzy's desk top. Mr. Average then proceeded to sit down at the desk and waved Izzy to a customer's chair. The office itself was a thing of beauty, having originally been built as a storage facility for important documents it was an addition to the main building with concrete reinforced walls and ceilings. With the advent of modern technology and the use of computers it had out lived its usefulness. Mr Sukinsin through the right contacts had been given the privilege of converting it to his private office. The walls had been refinished in a fine mahogany, a full bath had been added as well as a large screen TV. The finest carpets and furnishings completed it and it became a major status symbol for Mr Sukinsin. In the front of the office they had installed the pocket doors for additional security and when they were redoing the masonry they added 4 inch wide one way glass to both sides of the door. By tapering the brickwork to a substantial degree it became possible for the people inside the office to have an excellent view of the whole lobby.

Having settled themselves into their chairs Mr Average started to explain to Izzy the full details of the situation. "My name is Charles Richard Breumer and though the name means nothing to you now, before today is over you will know that name much better than you would ever wish to." "One thing I would like to impress on you at the onset is that I have been in the Army and served in Vietnam. I have killed people before and would have no problem shooting you! The bottom line is that I am holding a loaded 12 gauge shotgun and my service revolver is also on me. The situation simply put is, going back to an old "cliché" is that you currently have one foot on a banana peel and the other in the grave."

"We have a few hour session before us and it would be best for all concerned for you to realize that your thoughts and opinions are not worth a pinch of coonshit, I call the shots and when I say jump you should ask how high on your way up! The first item on the agenda will be to call your legal beagle Wilfred P Kisselbeak and give him this message exactly as I dictate it to you. I know he is in his office this morning for a few hours so you tell him simply that a very important issue has arisen and that it could have a major impact on both your lives. No details over the phone but if he could drop in for a few minutes it would be fantastic. Thank you."

Mr. Kisselbeak showed up less than fifteen minutes later and Charlie having the remote in his hand was able to see him and have the door slide open just as he arrived and it slid closed right on his heels. Kisselbeak looked puzzled to see Izzy sitting on a customer's chair and a stranger at the desk until he saw the weapons on the desk and then his awareness grew. Charlie motioned Kisselbeak to the other chair and when he had him settled in he proceeded to fully explain the situation to them. "You must realize that if you spend most of your time calling the tunes that the time will come when you must pay the piper. I am the self-appointed piper. I am sure that you will both be trying to excuse your actions as being business like and legitimate but I wish to make one point abundantly clear. This is my court and I am the judge! No attorneys, no escape clauses, no exceptions and my decision is final. Now the plaintiff will present his evidence as follows:

Myself and my wife Marion were reasonably comfortable in our paid for home. Having recently reached the right age and started receiving our pensions we were quite comfortable. Our biggest concern was that with our minimum pensions and after paying off our expenses there was basically nothing left. We had always hoped to do some travelling but with the rising costs the prospects seemed dim. Our three children, two girls and a son would not be able to help us as they were barely scraping by themselves. Then we saw Sukinsins ads in the local paper where his firm was looking for customers and would be paying between 15% to 20% interest yearly on the deposits. Having nothing but time on our hands, Marion and I made some enquiries into this proposal. The fact that we had no funds in hand was no problem we were assured because we could borrow money against our home, as it was paid for home. Doing the simple math and checking with our bank we could see that if we borrowed 40,000 at their rate of six and a half percent and if we only realized fifteen percent we could make a profit of 3,400 dollars per year which would give us enough spending money to take a nice trip every year. Being simple trusting folks we were like sheep being led to the slaughter. Within five months of our investment "which we had been informed later in the process was actually purchase of shares" in the investment firm we received a dividend cheque in the sum of 4,000 dollars which covered out interest and payment for a good part of the year. This investment seemed almost too good to be true. Towards the end of the first year we were contacted by your paper salesman that there were some awesome new prospects in the future, the hints of merging with a major investment firm which could mean that the value of our shares would jump substantially and the other prospective benefits. It was also pointed out that as preferred investors we would be given the opportunity to invest another 40,000 dollars with an ever increasing margin of profit. While we would not normally have even considered that amount of investment, the hook was into us so we proceeded to deal with our bank and took another mortgage on our house, a second mortgage at nine percent.

Halfway through the second year and with no further dividends arriving the pressure to make the payments became very difficult and eventually impossible to do. We made repeated calls to the office but were given assurance that everything was going along fine but that we would have to be patient for a while. Shortly after we were unable to talk to anyone at the office and could only leave messages which were never returned.

By now we began to realize that we had been had, but the sad part of the situation was that we were totally helpless to do anything about it. Then the roof caved in when we received a notice from our bank that due to major problems with payments they would have to foreclose on the property and could we please either pay the full balance owing or vacate the house within sixty days.

We rented a small apartment on the outskirts of town with just over half the living area, no yard and mostly Marion missed her garden and fruit trees. I missed my shop. When we had the house we also had our two pet poodles Tippy and Zoey and some of our finest times were to go for lengthy walks with them. They were the replacement family for the children who had left us. Any apartment we could find and afford would not allow pets. That was Marion's first devastating blow since we had to give them both away with the only concern being that they went to good homes.

The walks which we used to take a few times a day became shorter and less frequent until the time came that Marion hardly went walking anymore. My lone walks became shorter and shorter and many times when I returned I would find her on the lounge chair with a picture of our previous home on her lap. The picture is where she is on the grass with the dogs in her lap and the garden and fruit trees in the background. This had always been her favorite picture and she would be laying there with heartbreaking sadness on her face and the obvious stains of dried tears on her cheeks. She had always blamed herself for our misfortune for she said very emphatically that the only reason I had been willing to gamble at all was because I was trying to enrich her life with the travels. No amount of discussions would change her mind and she remained firmly convinced that it was all her fault.

The loss of her home, her pets, her trees and garden was like taking a beautiful growing flower and removing it from the life giving soil.

And then came the day when I returned from my lonesome walk to find her on the lounge chair in the living room. She had apparently laid down to rest and then her heavily burdened heart would beat no more. She had drifted off to a place where there were no tears, cheats or thieves and there could be a permanent peace for her there. I will tell you quite frankly that I was just a heartbeat away from joining her in her peaceful place. In the end the only thing that stopped me was the knowledge that having suffered an excruciating loss of their mother and grandmother the rest of the family would need all the help they could get in order to survive that blow.

"When I buried Marion I buried all my hopes and dreams and my future with her. Mr. Sukinsin and Mr. Kisselbeak you not only stole my money, lost me my home and in that process killed my wife. In my judgement you owe me 290 thousand dollars to be paid into an account of my choosing early this afternoon to dispose of as I see fit with no restrictions at all. Also in the process I will have you fill out your confessions to your crimes as per my instructions which we can all countersign and validate. You protest that it is not possible to accomplish this in that small amount of time. Well I intend to show you some shortcuts we will take in the process. In the meantime just sit back in your chairs. Keep your mouths shut and be prepared to follow instructions to the letter."

"You boys look tired and thirsty, well I'm happy to inform you that this is all part of the incentive plan and that as soon as this is satisfactorily over you can drink all you want." With that, Charlie fired up his cell phone and called a preprogrammed number.

"Good morning Sheriff's office, how may we help you" was the response.

"Is the Sheriff in please?"

"One moment Sir." And the silence for a couple of minutes and then Mickeys voice on the line.

"Good morning, Sheriff Mulcahey here, what can I do for you?"

"Good morning Mickey, this is Charlie Breumer. I don't know if you remember me, but you were at my house during my wife's passing and if I forgot to thank you then I would like to do so now, for your kindness and understanding."

"Yes, I remember you well Charlie and sorry again for your loss. How can I help you?"

"Mickey, I am sitting in the presence of I.M. Sukinsin and Wally Kisselbeak in Mr. Sukinsins office. They are two of the key people who set up the scam to swindle me and Marion of our money, resulting in the loss of our house and eventually my loss of her. They owe me according to my figures the sum of 290 thousand which they will pay me today or else they will have no tomorrow. I am sitting in

Izzy's fancy locked office with a sawed off 12 gauge shotgun and my old army service revolver as a guarantee that this will take place today."

"Izzy will phone his banker shortly and ask him to transfer enough money into his account to accomplish this and obviously he will be assured that this cannot be done in this short of time. I would like you to contact the banker that unless this is accomplished this day both Izzy and Kisselbeak will be dining tonight with the devil himself."

"Since Izzy's lawyer is here they can draw up any documentation on the office computer that they could possibly need. We will provide the banks with your phone number so that they could keep you informed so that you can hopefully provide incentives and help guide them through to a successful conclusion."

I think it would be best if the news media was kept out of the proceeding until after it is over and the account is paid in full."

There were some moments of silence and then the response came through loud and clear.

"I follow what you're doing Charlie and although it is totally unlawful and illegal I will try to get this through as soon as we can and hopefully nobody gets hurt.

With that cooperative assurance he instructed Izzy to contact his banker personally and explain the situation and ask for his utmost cooperation. In the meantime Kesselbeak was provided with a handy laptop and directed to provide the document for their later signature.

Their confessions were as follows:

I Izreal Micheal Sukinsin do admit my guilt in engineering a pyramid scheme set up in order to steal money from innocent people and I do acknowledge my responsibility to my heirs and assigns to return as much of this money as they possibly can.

Signed:

I Wilfred P. Kisselbeak do admit my guilt of being involved in the pyramid scheme and would give permission to the courts to access any of the assets to repay those innocent people to the utmost degree.

Signed:

While they were sitting there Charlie seemed very relaxed in his chair and almost falling asleep. Izzy, unhappy with the situation started contemplating the options of Charlie dozing off and him being able to rush Charlie and overpower him. As he was glancing around at his best course of action his eyes focused back on Charlie and he found himself staring at the pistol sighted right between his eyes. Then he heard the soft click of the hammer being cocked and felt a cold chill run down his back and a rush of diarrhea over take him. He heard Charlie's soft voice admonish him, "that was a close one."

To prevent any further problems or delays he allowed Izzy the opportunity to go to the washroom and relieve himself. Since the bathroom faced the office desk, with the doors left open he could easily monitor the whole situation. Meanwhile Izzy had any thought of rebellion driven from his mind.

As expected the response from Izzys banker was that there wasn't enough money in his current account and that generating that sum would take time and effort including substantial financial commitment from the both of them. With the almost certain prospect of no tomorrow unless the money was forthcoming Izzy proceeded to inform his banker of substantial moneys kept in other formerly hidden accounts overseas registered in various limited corporations and easily available to him. He provided the information with reluctance aware that there would be not only other creditors interested in that information but also government taxation agencies.

When his banker did confirm that the necessary funds were available he proceeded to fax to us the necessary documents involved in the proposed transfer. The trapped rats were very helpful in the paperwork in the hope that they could be completed as soon as possible and that they could be set free. By the time of one thirty the paperwork was done and faxed back from the bank that the sun of 290,000 was to be credited to the account of Charlie's choosing. The boys were sadly disappointed that this was not the end of the episode but only the first phase.

Having received a faxed copy of this bank balance Charlie proceeded to the next step. On his cell phone he entered the number of his oldest child, his daughter Brenda and was happy to hear her soft voice on the phone. "Hello there."

"Brenda, good afternoon this is your father and how are you and the children?"

She and her husband Thomas had two children, Alan 14 and Bailey 11.

"Oh Dad, I am so happy to hear from you, it's been quite a few weeks and we were worried sick about you. The children are fine but lonesome for you, they are in school now but they will be thrilled to know you are ok. What's up with you?"

"Brenda, you will be happy to hear, that through a stroke of good fortune I have recently come into some money. I will explain all the details later but meanwhile I shall be transferring to Thomas and yourself the sum of $290,000.00 and it will be there shortly. Check with your banker and as soon as it is there have him transfer $95,000.00 of that money through to pay off your mortgage, which I know is almost that, then call your brother Alan and transfer another $95,000.00 to his account to pay off his mortgage also. Next you must get a hold of Melissa and transfer the same amount to her and tell her to pay off any debts she has and take anything extra out in cash. Withdraw any remaining money in your accounts and take it home as cash for now. Be sure you all get receipts for your transactions. If any banks try to delay anything please call Sheriff Mulcahey at this number, explain the situation and let him straighten them out. I would like this done as speedily as possible for reasons which will be obvious later. Please have everyone phone you when they are done and then please phone me at the number I will provide. I hope I hear from you soon, I love you all and goodbye for now."

With all that underway he proceeded to relax a bit,

and encouraged his captives to complete their confessions properly and as soon as possible. Noticing that Izzy had been sweating profusely for some time and that he was getting quite fidgety Charlie allowed them to take a turn using the washroom, and since there was bottled water there he let them take a bottle each for refreshment but cautioned them to make it last for the next one could be a long time coming. Having rummaged through Izzy's desk earlier, he had discovered an almost full bottle of imported Canadian Crown Royal Whiskey. Pouring himself a small glass he was pleased to discover that this was a prime sipping whiskey, but not wanting the alcohol to have an impact on his performance he was very careful with his consumption. During his wait he had been in touch with Mickey and he had suggested to him that time being of an essence he could touch base with the bankers regarding the children's accounts and ask for their utmost co-operation through these difficult times. He was assured by Mickey that he was ahead of the game, having been in touch with everyone that could possibly help and that everyone was already online.

Charlie, having been concerned that there could be major delays was pleasantly surprised when he received a call from Brenda shortly before 4:30 that although her brother and sister were puzzled by the events happening they had been successful on their end, receipts in hand and waiting for further info.

Pouring himself another 2 ounces of Izzy's excellent whiskey Charlie proceeded to address his two very unhappy partners to inform them of the situation as it now stood. "Obviously throughout this process you could have reasonably assumed that once we were done here you would be allowed to go home to your comfortable residences and that your life would go on as before. If you received that impression from me either through my comments or actions I make no apologies, I lied! In your lifestyles and your professions that was obviously something that you did on a daily basis is lie, this is the only reason you managed to cheat not only me but hundreds of others out of their life savings."

While the two of them were digesting that ominous sounding message Charlie picked up his phone and went to the far corner of the room to have a private talk with Mickey, "Mickey these two bastards have hurt a lot of people so before this is over I intend to scare the shit out of them, so if you hear a few shots do not be alarmed for that is a clear sign that we are almost at the end of this process. A few minutes after the shots I will have the door slide open and when you walk in you will find me in the chair at the desk with the weapon well out of reach. I want to thank you very much for without your help we could not have peacefully resolved this issue." With that he turned back to his captives with more devastating news. "I am from the old school of thought where if you took a pound of butter off the shelf you were obliged to pay the full price if you wished to buy the butter, In my court if you take a life you must also pay a life… or two! In this case, if you know any prayers perhaps this is the time to say them."

While they sat there frozen Charlie picked up his service revolver and as if almost by magic, with a loud clap of thunder a neat hole appeared in the forehead of Isreal Micheal Sukinsin, centered almost exactly between his eyes. Izzy's body arched up for a few seconds and then slammed back against the wall and slowly slid down into his chair, remaining there at a strange angle. Kisselbeak, terrorized and in panic stood up partly from his chair and then the first bullet caught him in the chest which froze him temporarily till the second bullet pierced his left hand shirt pocket, his cell phone and then his heart, leaving a text message on the wall composed in blood, flesh and cell phone parts that Wilfred P Kisselbeak had now permanently retired and would cheat no more!

Charlie proceeded to lay his weapons on a small coffee table some ways from the desk and then sat down and poured himself a rather large helping of the whiskey. Halfway through the drink he pressed the button to allow the pocket doors to slide open so that the Sheriff could make his way into the room. There was total disbelief in the Sheriffs eyes when upon entering the room, there was Charlie, totally relaxed and sipping the last of the whiskey. The weapons were well out of reach as he had stated they would be, but the two carcasses slumped in the chairs across the room made for a shocking sight.

"Sorry if I misled you" was Charlie's first response to the Sheriff "but I did tell you I would scare the shit out of them and by the smell of the room that prediction was totally accurate."

The Sheriff then began the standard procedure of arresting Charlie, cuffing him and reading him his rights before loading him up and taking him off to jail. The next item was to wait for the arrival of the coroner and his examination of the scene before he could release the bodies for removal. Then began the grisly task of removing the bodies to the morgue, of photographing and gathering of evidence before sealing off the office for further examinations.

Throughout the interrogation process they were surprised at the degree of co-operation from Charlie and also how well he had planned the whole scheme. When questioned about the assassination of his two captives and as to whether that was part of the plan or not he had a very simple explanation, he had hoped for and was extremely happy to recover his money mainly for his children's sake but he had every intention to shoot both of his victims (or as he referred to them, scum). And as far as he was concerned there were at least two very good reasons. One reason being based on his philosophy of an eye for an eye. They had destroyed his wife, his life and the happiness of his family and should pay with their lives. The second and equally important reason was the fact that they had signed confessions of their crimes and if left to live they would, with their many resources have denied the confessions and tried to get my money back. Therefore with them out of the way for good, that wouldn't happen, there would be an option for other victims of their scams to try to recover some of their money from the estates of the two criminals.

His final comments at the end of the interrogation brought smiles to more than a few of the people watching the interview. "Those two bastards caused me a lot of pain and grief and lack of sleep, but tonight I'm going to sleep like a baby and they are going to have a long "sleep" too. My darling wife can now rest in peace."

The news headlines the next day were very graphic
"Scam Artists Cheat Many But Not The Devil"
"Monster In Jail Charged With First Degree Murder"
"Downtown Office, Scene Of Terrible Crime"
"Charlie Will Need His Angels To Help Him"

"Crime Does Not Pay"

The news headlines had hardly died down when Sheriff Mickey Mulcahey had a surprise visitor. A young and enterprising lawyer named Andy Knute Svabodnik asked if he could speak to Charlie. He was advised that Charlie was not looking for a defence lawyer but pressed the Sheriff to urge Charlie to allow him a few minutes to discuss his charges.

His message to Charlie was short and concise "You have done something that the majority of people feel is long overdue and you may feel satisfied and be prepared to spend the rest of your life in jail, but I want you to think of your family's loss and the unhappiness it will be causing them. Let's go a step further and use your actions to make people more aware of the danger of dealing with similar individuals and the scams they perpetrate on the unsuspecting victims. We can use the anger and outrage of the people to not only inflict a greater punishment on that type of person, and I also feel we can use those same sentiments to help you to a very great degree."

"I believe that what you have done was morally right and I am prepared to defend you pro bono. In fact I will be honest in saying that the exposure will bring me a lot of good publicity" Before he left Andy and Charlie shook hands and entered into an agreement that Charlie had acquired himself legal counsel. It would soon become apparent that Charlie had what proved to be a Cracker Jack lawyer and it may have been one of the smartest moves Charlie had made in his recent past.

When the legal procedures commenced and Charlie was formally indicted before the Judge Andy came up with a proposal to the court. His strongest argument being that with the deed already been done Charlie posed no further risk to the community or himself. In no way, shape or form was Charlie a danger to Society and since there was no prospect of Charlie trying to escape the system would save thousands of tax dollars on his further incarceration. He then requested that Charlie be released on bail until his trial. There was major opposition to bail from the prosecutors as this was without question a double murder with premeditation, so it was obviously murder in the 1st degree. Mainly to accede to their legitimate concerns the Judge granted bail at an amount most considered too high for Charlie to afford, $750,000.00 Interestingly enough most people assumed that Charlie would be staying in jail until his trial, but lo and behold there was the owner of a car dealership with more than enough assets who immediately put up the bail money. It became known that one of his children had also been stung by Izzy and his scams. Andy began using the Media to Charlie's advantage, he began to make people more aware of Charlie's great suffering, his tragic loss of his wife and his home and his desperate efforts to make things right. Not only for himself but for others who were victims of the same scam artists.

Almost out of the blue small donations of money started pouring in through the mail. Sums of $5.00 to $100.00 in letters addressed to Charlie Breumer, all with the desire to help him in this fight for his freedom. Charlie's response which was both predictable and beautiful was that since he had recovered his monetary loss that any money coming in would go into a special account so that the other legitimate victims of Izzy's scam could also recover some or all of their money too.

Andy, shrewd bugger that he was, set it up so that the bankers would take nothing and Andy who would do most of the paperwork along with a small committee would also receive no monies from the account. This would ensure that 100% of the money would go only to the victims, resulting in a huge amount of positive publicity directed towards both Charlie and Andy. When this information became public the flood of donations increased dramatically.

A very reluctant Charlie, was drawn by an opportunistic Andy, into some very emotional town meetings where afterwards Charlie was treated by the average person as a hero. The many compliments and assurances of support almost brought Charlie to tears.

While Charlie was trying to cope with all that was happening, his son in law being in a much better financial situation than before had begun renovations in his basement on a small self-contained suite for Charlie. This would allow Charlie to spend more time with his family especially the grand children while still allowing him the privacy he deserved. The very interesting part of this is that when the neighbors became aware of the renovations the flow of donations of materials and labour to complete the project was food for the soul. When the day came for Charlie to inspect and occupy his new digs there was a surprise welcoming party for him arranged by the people in the neighborhood.

In the meantime Andy had been managing to postpone the trial date not only to provide Charlie with the opportunity to spend much more time with his family but also to allow more time for people to think about his actions and realize that he was not the cold blooded murderer that some of the media had portrayed him to be. It provided the chance for people to see that he was just a poor individual like any of them who having been bilked out of his hard earned money, and who had been driven by circumstances to try to recover his money and bring about a moral justice into the game for everyone.

The time finally came about almost 6 months later that Andy really proved his worth, when he began to negotiate with the Prosecutors in regards to the charges laid against Charlie. He stated to them that unless the charge of 1st degree murder were greatly reduced he would have his client plead that he acted in self defense since they were trying to destroy him. He reminded them that with the people as a whole supportive of Charlie, the prosecution might have a difficult time trying to get a jury to convict him of murder in the 1st. He also reminded them that all he needed to do was convince one or two members of any jury that Charlie had acted in self defence to save his own life and sanity and he could expect a hung jury and that further trials could be even more difficult to prosecute.

After a private meeting it became evident that the prosecutor shared Andy's thinking as the charge of murder in the 1st was offered to be changed to 1st degree manslaughter. Andy would have none of that and eventually the charge was mutually agreed upon as 2nd degree manslaughter. The prosecution also agreed not to make any sentencing recommendations but to leave that up to the Judge to decide.

As the trial got under way Andy waited for the

prosecution to present their side of the case without many interruptions or delays. When the prosecution had closed Andy rose and stood before the jury, his boyish appearance a simple demeanor was an asset to him for he seemed to be an honest and sincere man.

He began his address to the jury "The prosecution is trying to present my client, the defendant as some kind of monster who mercilessly concocted a scheme to destroy two wonderful people. On the contrary it becomes abundantly clear that here is a kind and gentle man who has lived his life as the finest neighbor you could have. I can bring you if necessary any number of character witnesses as to his qualities. He will walk his neighbor's dog, he drives everyone's children when their own parents can't to sporting events, he has taken the church groups children camping, usually at his own expense. He has volunteered for every imaginable charity or fund drive. In fact if there were a contest in this area for the most kind hearted and beloved member of the community Charlie would win it with no sweat. I make these statements to you without corroboration but I will invite the prosecution to dispute any of these statements and then provide the evidence to support their position."

"Charlie is your neighbor, your son, your best friend a solid citizen who fought for his country through the war in Vietnam. He bore no ill will to anyone and wanted only to live with the love of his life Marion and with the companionship of his children and grandchildren. When we talk or think about monsters than let us look at Sukinsin and Kisselbeak. They lived a good and comfortable life but it didn't have enough frills and extra benefits so instead of working harder or being wiser in order to improve their lifestyle they engineered a scam. It doesn't take that much skill to accomplish that when you are dealing with honest, trusting people. They knew, without question, that people would be destroyed by their scam and that lives could be lost. Did they care? Not worth a damn! These weren't people they were dealing with, to them they were sheep waiting to be led to slaughter. There is no question as to who were in fact the monsters in this instance."

It is an obvious fact that through their machinations they did cause him to lose his life savings, his lifestyle and there should be no question in anyone's mind that they killed his wife!"

"Now murder is a very broad term and we all know that there are many ways to murder someone. Now the one in this situation is to take away everything that would give a person the desire to keep on living. Now we are left with someone it could be me, it could be you, who has lost everything in his innocence because of another's greed or lack of concern. The situation is simply this, under those circumstances some people will just roll over and die, you can't fight the system. But there are other people like Charlie who have gambled their life and fought for this countries freedom, who will say NO, this is not acceptable and proceed to do something about it. He attempted to not only recover his loss but also to punish those who would do these evil deeds. Hopefully to discourage others from doing that wrong to people. I want every one of you on the jury to look back into your soul and honestly say that you see Charlie as a monster, or just a reflection of yourself in his circumstances. The prosecution has never stated that Charlie did it for greed, and that is obvious to us all. He did what he had to do in order to be able to live with himself.

When you do your debating I ask for only one thing, never mind how the law looks at it but remember that there is some space between legal and moral justice. Just judge Charlie as if you had his life to live and as how you would react. Thank you."

Since many of the facts were documented and obvious, and with Charlie not denying his execution of Sukinsin and Kisselbeak the trial came to a fairly quick conclusion. The jury deliberations were also fairly quick but although the verdict was guilty there was a very strong recommendation from the jury that whatever the sentence it should be a suspended one. This was based on the fact that he was obviously no threat to society but that also his continuing efforts to help other victims of fraud would be better served if he were not in jail. The judge well aware of the public sentiment came up with a suspended sentence of five years.

It was a beautiful day on the fourteenth of October which was the day of Charlie's seventieth birthday party the whole family had gathered together at Charlie's pad including a few neighbours, and of course Andy was there. In the midst of the celebrations Andy presented Charlie with a very important document. Notification that the governor, Yuri P. Statlukin had issued Charlie a full pardon, citing as some of the reasons being that some of Charlie's actions were caused by circumstances beyond his control. But the main reason being that Charlie was on a new path bringing honor to himself and the community and providing an example for others to follow.

Nobody knew that weeks before Andy had a short private session with Yuri and since Yuri was trailing in the polls with an election only weeks away Andy had suggested that Yuri might be wise to piggy back on Charlie's popularity. This was mainly the reason that Andy was able to bring such a welcome present to the birthday party.

It was a fine day and the party was one of the finest

around and the grand finale came when five year old Sammy climbed onto his grandfather's lap, giving him a massive hug and said with tears streaming from his eyes, "we lost grandma and we loved her very very much, but we still have you. I love you grandpa." The conglomeration of children and grandchildren also attempted to hug and kiss Charlie which was food for the soul.

As Charlie leaned back in his easy chair relaxed and comfortable he looked around at the love and happiness being shared by everyone, and he felt, not even knowing how he felt it, in fact he knew it, Marion was there! She was in the smiles of the people who were almost strangers. She was in the smiles and laughter of the children, both ours and theirs. She was in the love that saturated the whole area and finally he could sense that she was totally at peace not only with herself, but also the rest of the world. He did not know why or how she came; he could only know that she came. Maybe it was all the love and happiness in the place that was like a psychic magnet that dragged her there. And when later on things normalized and she faded away, he had no way to know if she would return or not, but why wouldn't she for the love magnet was there to stay. And he could feel a soft warm glow through his body almost as if to say that Charlie didn't have to worry whether he could ever get to heaven or not. Heaven had come to Charlie it was a glorious day!

Backword

YURI P. STATLUKIN WON the gubernatorial race by a margin of almost two to one. We believe that if Andrew Knute Svabodnik ever entered into politics he could go a long way.

www.ingramcontent.com/pod-product-compliance
Lightning Source LLC
Chambersburg PA
CBHW051601120626
46551CB00013B/1623